Jeff Gordon
On A Chance

Maureen Harris

Jeff Gordon On A Chance
Copyright © 2016 by Maureen Harris

HOBO PUBLISHING

Maureen Harris © photography may not be copied by any means, nor to another computer, transmitted, published, reproduced, stored, manipulated, projected, or altered in any way, including without limitation any digitization or synthesizing of the images, alone or with any other material, by use of computer or other electronic means or any other method or means now or hereafter known, without the written permission of Maureen Harris and arrangement thereof. No images are within Public Domain. Use of any image as the basis for another photographic concept or illustration is a violation of copyright. All photographs, text appearing in this book, or any other Maureen Harris publications are the exclusive intellectual property of Maureen Harris and are protected under United States and International copyright laws. Maureen Harris vigorously protects copyright interests. By purchasing and viewing this work you are agreeing to be bound by the terms of this agreement.

All rights reserved. No part of this book may be used or reproduced in any manner whatsoever without written permission except in the case of brief quotations embodied in critical articles and reviews.

Jeff Gordon On A Chance previously published as Opening Jeff Gordon's Mail.

Printed in the United States of America by
HOBO PUBLISHING
www.hobopublishing.com

Library of Congress Control Number: 2016917479
ISBN: 978-0-9829206-5-7

Table of Contents

Foreword
Acknowledgements
Personal Touch Fan Club
Fan Mail
Personal Experiences
JGNFC Collectibles

Maureen Harris ~ Jeff ~ Russ Harris

Foreword

A random letter began the chance of a lifetime for Jeff Gordon fans Maureen and Russ Harris, when they founded the Jeff Gordon National Fan Club, the largest personal touch fan base in the history of NASCAR. If you sent a letter to Jeff Gordon in the 1990's, chances are that it was processed by the JGNFC.

From the outset, they catered not just to the fans of Jeff Gordon, but all race fans. By doing so, they created the most popular fan connection in all of racing during the 1990's.

Jeff Gordon On A Chance will take you inside the JGNFC and give insight into the Jeff Gordon fan. Also, Maureen shares some humorous "fanatics" that she and Russ went through as not only JGNFC founders but as simple fans.

I hope that as a race fan you will appreciate the unique experiences that the Harrises were fortunate to have. It was a dream come true for two ordinary fans to be involved in the rise of a racing superstar.

Above:
Russ Harris & Jeff

Right:
Russ Harris in
the #24 Pit.

Acknowledgements

First and foremost, I would like to thank God, without whom none of this could have happened.

Second, I would like to express my thanks to my wonderful husband Russ. What a blessing in life to have been involved in such a satisfying opportunity as the Jeff Gordon National Fan Club, while sharing all the joy and fun of racing with my best friend. When this book was just a thought, Russ became ill and later succumbed in his fight with cancer, and returned home to spirit. I dedicate this book, in honor of Russ.

A big thank you to all the members of the JGNFC for all your support and friendship for more than a decade that you shared the Jeff Gordon National Fan Club with us. We truly were a family of fans!

Special thanks to Jeff, as well as to Carol, and John Bickford for giving Russ and me a chance of a lifetime. We had such a blast being involved in the sport we both loved so much, which included meeting some of racing's best fans, and sharing our favorite driver. The memories will last forever.

Thanks again, Jeff, for such a sweet ride!

Personal Touch Fan Club

Our chance of a lifetime started simply as two motorsport fans. We began watching 16-year-old Jeff Gordon drive those big Open Wheel sprint cars. Russ and I were attracted to Jeff during his open wheel days as we watched him on ESPN's *Thursday Night Thunder*. Gosh, we couldn't wait for the nights when he was racing. His all out racing style, which is indicative of open wheel, continued once he stepped into stock cars. A dominant and talented young man, Jeff Gordon had the presence of a born-to-race driver.

In 1991, I wrote Jeff a letter inquiring about his fan club, and also if it was possible to get photos of his race car as reference for building a model. At the time we wrote the letter, Jeff had just entered into stock cars, and was running a limited amount of open wheel races.

Upon writing our letter, we searched everywhere for his address. All we could come up with was that Jeff and his family lived in Pittsboro, Indiana. Our letter was addressed simply: Jeff Gordon, Driver, Carolina Ford Dealers #1, Pittsboro, Indiana 46167. Jeff's mother, Carol Bickford, was

First time meeting our favorite driver Jeff Gordon. Maureen & Russ Harris with Jeff at Phoenix Raceway. (1992)

1 *Jeff Gordon: On A Chance*

Jeff in Phoenix Raceway garage area during the Copper World Classic. (1992)

Jeff Gordon: On A Chance 2

touched that the letter had reached them with no physical address and also that I wanted to build a model of her son's race car. She picked up the phone and called us. Of course, we had put our phone number in the letter!

In our telephone conversation, Carol informed us that Jeff would be driving a sprint car in the Phoenix Copper World Classic at Phoenix International Raceway (PIR). If we could *hook up* with them at the track, we could discuss the fan club. She also said it would be a good time to get some photos. We agreed to meet them at the racetrack.

Once we arrived at PIR we got together with Jeff, his mom, and step-dad, John Bickford, in the garage area. It was really cool because in those days we were able to drive our vehicle down into the garage area located near Jeff's pit.

If you have ever been to a racetrack, "catch is as catch can," as the saying goes. It becomes a full day of standing around and watching a bunch of people fuss over a piece of machinery. But then, the engine fires up, the driver heads onto the track, and it's all worth the wait! Speed and racing – what a super high!

During a lunch break in between practices and working on the race car, Jeff's mom came and told us that it was a good time to talk with John who was managing Jeff at the time. So, she escorted Russ and I inside the race trailer. I will never forget seeing Jeff's step-dad sitting on a bunch of tires while eating lunch. As Russ and John talked, Russ handed John a hand sketched mock-up of the newsletter. John placed it on his knee and kept eating while reviewing the newsletter. Finally, he said, "I like it, let's do it, provided of course that Jeff likes it. Hang around and I'll talk with Jeff." Of course, where were we going? We both loved being in the garage, as opposed to sitting in the stands. So much more goes on down here, giving us a backseat view of motorsports.

We milled around, looking at the other race cars, and were fortunate enough to meet some of the drivers. We were also able to take lots of photos of Jeff's race car so if they said yes, we would have plenty of photos to use in our publication. Soon Carol came and said, "John would like to see you." We went back to Jeff's race trailer where John told us he showed the newsletter to Jeff and that Jeff liked the idea, and asked us to begin working on it right away. Carol gave us their phone numbers and addresses and said we would get together later over the phone to discuss the details.

We stayed around the garage the rest of the afternoon, took many more photos, watched the races, went to several driver appearances, at one of which we met Davey Allison, and just had a great weekend of racing. There were comical moments as well. I'll never forget the time we went to an appearance that Jeff and several other drivers were scheduled to attend. The event was located at a local restaurant/bar. Since Jeff was underage, his parents had to accompany him. He was old enough to race the huge race cars but not old enough to enter a bar for an appearance. It made us chuckle.

After talking with Jeff and his parents in Phoenix, it was agreed that we would produce and publish a monthly newsletter for all 43 members of Jeff's fan club. We started with an 8 page monthly newsletter run off on a copy machine, which would soon grow into a 16 page newsletter, dedicated strictly to the fans.

How did we find so much to write about one driver? That's easy. When you have someone as popular as Jeff Gordon, his fans want to know every detail about him, including what he is doing, what he likes, what he eats, and when he sneezes. Well, you get the idea. Those who are not *die-hard* race fans have to understand the addiction of the fans' support to their favorite drivers in the world of racing.

The newsletter was created in house, and took about two weeks to produce. Once it was returned from the printer, our office labeled and stamped each newsletter and then delivered them to the local post office. Over the years, as the membership within the club grew, we were mailing such great amounts of the ever popular newsletter that it required the use of our truck to transport the stacks to the post office.

Jeff, we're glad you made the switch from open wheel to stock cars!

Above: Jeff at a driver appearance in Phoenix, AZ, after racing in the Copper World Classic. (1992)

5   *Jeff Gordon: On A Chance*

Russ Harris with Jeff and crew his chief Ray Evernham at Phoenix Raceway.

Soon after we started producing the club newsletter, we were asked to take over all of the fan club operations. After acquiring the entire fan club operation, we began handling the processing of Jeff's ever increasing fan mail of a non-legal nature. Right off of turn one, Jeff wanted his club to have a personal touch and thus the Jeff Gordon National Fan Club was born. With the assistance of Jeff and his parents we were able to build one of the largest personal touch fan clubs in the history of NASCAR.

We took the words fan club and turned it into Fan Relations in order to provide the personalization that would include every member as part of the 24 team. As fans ourselves, we knew the passion other fans had towards Jeff, so it was easier for us to relate to his fan base.

When Jeff entered stock cars at a young age, his contribution of youth helped the sport achieve greater exposure, and the club began to explode in popularity. Russ and I decided that we no longer enjoyed living in the large city of Phoenix. So we headed up to northern Arizona, where we loved to camp and happened to fall in love with the little town of Williams, Arizona. No stop lights, traffic, and an enviable quality of life. We asked about the fan club moving to Williams, and everyone agreed that with modern technology, it could be located just about anywhere. Therefore, off we went, moving the growing club to northern Arizona.

Russ and I were astounded by the driver's *star status* due to the booming interest in racing at the time. We spent hour after hour communicating with fans and bringing them joy through the love of their favorite driver. The fan club provided us an opportunity to assist Jeff in touching many lives of not only his devoted JGNFC members, but all race fans as well.

The JGNFC became an unprecedented fan base which published a 16-page monthly newsletter, and provided six personalized fan club events each year throughout the country, in which Jeff would appear. Every fan club member received a personalized autographed driver postcard and other special goodies in their fan club packet.

Our family of fans consisted of some of the most wonderful people that we have ever met. Russ and I were truly blessed to have been associated with each and every one of them; and to have played a small part in bringing happiness, hope, love, and faith, through racing and Jeff Gordon, into the lives of so many race fans.

At one fan club event a member conveyed to Russ how lucky he was to be associated with Jeff. Russ responded how honored we were to be in a position that allowed us to participate in Jeff's operation. But in the whole scheme of things we were far down on the "totem pole". The member replied, "Yea, but at least you are on the pole!"

Jeff's fan mail during the first year was not as varied as in the later *stardom* years. Notice I said *stardom*, because that is what the NASCAR drivers of today have become in the eyes of the fan, superstars. We believe due to the fact that race car drivers are in the public eye a constant eleven months out of twelve, they have become not just drivers but an addiction, star quality personalties.

Maureen Harris assisting Jeff at an autograph appearance in North Carolina.

7   *Jeff Gordon: On A Chance*

The JGNFC grew from 43 members to thousands in such a short period of time, during which, there was never a downturn in the membership. Even when we raised the membership fee well above other clubs, and were told it was a wrong decision by those clubs, we never saw a decrease in the membership. But soon those other clubs would follow suit.

Under Jeff's direction, we set up a series of fan club events across the country making the events open only to a certain number of members, in effect, giving Jeff the opportunity to meet his fans one on one. During the years of the JGNFC, Jeff set a precedent by providing the most fan club events to his fan club members.

Starting with four events, they immediately grew to six per year, held all across the country. Each meeting consisted of just 200 members, giving every member who attended a chance to meet Jeff. Because of the demand and interest in meeting Jeff, we soon created a lottery type drawing for event tickets from the members interested in attending a fan club meeting. This worked out well and gave a fair shake to all the members.

Russ Harris and Jeff at a JGNFC event.

With the influx of members, Russ and I decided to break up the fan club into regions. After creating JGNFC regions, we enlisted volunteer members to act as coordinators of these regions. Each regional coordinator was given the opportunity to run a JGNFC event if it occurred within their area. With an intimate group of fans attending the meetings, it allowed the regional coordinators and members a chance to visit with Jeff on a personal level.

I'm amazed that still with all

Jeff Gordon: On A Chance

JGNFC first Fan Club Event in Michigan, August 23, 1993.

After answering questions at the FCE, Jeff took a photograph with every member in attendance.

Above: Love the intent look of the baby towards Jeff! Already a fan!

9 *Jeff Gordon: On A Chance*

his success, and all of the pressures, Jeff is still Jeff. The same Jeff that showed up to fan club events, laid back -- just like his fans. The fans appreciated the chance to meet Jeff this way.

We also had great speakers at our events, such as Rick Hendrick, Ray Evernham, Ned Jarrett, Randy Pemberton, Sam Bass, Max Helton, and Benny Parsons, to name a few. The fan club events were a highlight for Russ and me, as it gave us a chance to meet face to face with so many of the great fans we communicated with via mail or by phone. It always seemed that everyone enjoyed the events, including Jeff.

One of our regional coordinators began an annual "Coast to Coast" fan club event. Several times a year, she would coordinate fan club meetings across the country where everyone attending, including non JGNFC members, would watch the race at the same time, communicating with each other via the internet. Thus, we created the only, Coast to Coast Fan Club Events. Our members were truly a family of fans. What fun!

Along with the fan club events, a monthly 16-page newsletter, a place to call and talk Jeff Gordon, the JGNFC changed the way drivers related to the members of their fan clubs. The JGNFC actually became the place where not only Jeff Gordon fans could call or write for information, but also became known by fans throughout racing as the place to receive information regarding any driver or happening in the world of racing. If we didn't know, we would find out for them. Our office

Maureen Harris and Jeff at a JGNFC Event.

Jeff Gordon: On A Chance 10

JGNFC Event Speakers

Above: Rick Hendrick
Middle: Broadcaster, Randy Pemberton
Below: Ned Jarrett, NASCAR Hall of Famer.

Above: John Bickford

Below: Max Helton from Motor Racing Outreach.

11 *Jeff Gordon: On A Chance*

Russ & Maureen Harris present Randy Pemberton with a gift.

soon became the racing fan's fan club.

Fans are very important to race car drivers. However, the drivers were getting so busy with the surge of popularity in motorsports, that they didn't have the proper amount of time to devote to organize, and keep their clubs running. We entered an area where fan clubs were run mostly by moms, sisters, or other family members and turned them into an operation catering strictly to the fans.

Jeff had the distinction of having the #1 history-making personal touch fan club in all of NASCAR. Under our direction, we changed the way NASCAR fan clubs were run, from the mom and pop type club of just answering fan mail, or by the non-personal corporations. We turned the JGNFC into a professional operation of *"fan relations."* The JGNFC provided a service to Jeff's fans and allowed the #24 family of fans a place to keep up with their love of racing and their favorite driver. It seemed we had found that sweet spot for creating a balance between providing a fan club and having an operation that could sustain itself. And we did it all without losing that personal touch.

As the mail for Jeff continued piling in, it became more than the two of us could handle. We soon had to hire extra office staff. Jeff would tease us that we had more employees than he did in his office. Russ joked with him and said, "Maybe

Maureen & Russ Harris with MRO's Max Helton at a JGNFC Fan Club Event.

Jeff Gordon: On A Chance

we do more work than you do." Of course, Jeff chuckled at that comment. (Whew! Glad Jeff has a sense of humor.)

By now, the internet had come into play and we were receiving 200 e-mails a day in addition to the thousands of pieces of mail each week. The devotion of his early die-hard fans, word of mouth in the stands, coupled with Jeff's popularity, resulted in the JGNFC rapidly expanding into the most popular fan based club in NASCAR racing. The members were from all walks of life, various ages, youth and adults alike; men and women, foreign members, and entire families. Some were fans who wouldn't admit in public they were members of the club! We also saw a lot of letters reflecting on the many newcomers to the sport of racing, which, in our opinion, had a lot to do with this new kid on the block.

Ray Evernham and Jeff at a JGNFC Fan Club Event.

The growth of motorsports programming on TV accelerated the popularity of the sport, yet that exposure did not take away from the one-on-one fan association with the driver. We had many families that were members of the JGNFC and other drivers' clubs, which made for great dinner conversation and race day antics. Fans often told us of the competition among family members as they gathered to watch the weekly races, and how each person with their own favorite driver would tease whomever was not having a good race day.

The JGNFC was housed in a large building which had some extra space. The idea came about to offer a history of Jeff's early racing career and create the JGNFC Museum. Through the help of John Bickford, we were able to display items chronicling the early years of Jeff's career.

Some items that were displayed in the JGNFC Museum were Jeff's first racing jacket he wore at age 5, early uniforms, helmets, trophies, and other personal items of his. The fans that ventured to the museum were treated to some special items of interest from Jeff's personal memorabilia. It was fun to share these unique items with the fans.

As Jeff's mail continued its steady growth, the JGNFC spent countless hours on behalf of Jeff writing and e-mailing fans in response to their correspondence.

Benny Parsons signing an autograph for a JGNFC member at a fan club event.

We never lost that personal touch, which often included taking the time to answer a call from any fan that had a question. We were always able to balance the burgeoning fan club tasks and still keep the incredible level of customer service available to the fans.

Our uncanny rapport with Jeff was what I believe assisted in the growth of the JGNFC. When we took over the club, it was on a hand shake deal, the old fashioned way of doing business. We gave Jeff our word that we would represent him to the best of our abilities. In turn, he supported pretty

Jeff Gordon: On A Chance

The JGNFC Museum displayed items from Jeff's early years in racing through his climb into the NASCAR Cup series.

Items on loan from the Gordon family at the JGNFC Museum included Jeff's first leather racing jacket (on left in above photo), and his first racing uniform (pictured in the middle of above photo).

Jeff and Russ Harris at the race track.

much whatever direction we wanted to go with the club.

Jeff was excited about his fans running his club, putting into it what the fans wanted. He gave us unprecedented support in taking the JGNFC the direction that would become the model for stock car racing fan clubs and several other celebrity fan clubs. Russ was always gracious in assisting with advice to other top notch race car drivers' fan clubs as well as other fan clubs outside of racing. He never hesitated to share the construction of the JGNFC as a self supporting venue. As a result, he was constantly asked for advice on how the JGNFC came to be the outstanding personal touch club that it was.

History will show that Jeff has gone on to become one of the greatest drivers of all time. Russ and I were proud to have made history ourselves as we took the membership of fans and created a system of fan relations that would be the model for personal touch racing fan clubs for many years to come.

After more than 10 wonderful years with the Jeff Gordon National Fan Club, Jeff wanted his fan club to move to the Charlotte, North Carolina area into his newly built shop. We were offered the opportunity to move there and continue with the club. However, we loved northern Arizona and our family was here, so we declined to move with the fan club. We are honored and blessed that Jeff and his folks gave us the opportunity to participate in the world of NASCAR racing in such a positive manner.

To this day, we still have the *fuel of racing* in our blood and will always consider Jeff near and dear to our hearts. He is the neatest race car driver ever and just an overall fine human being.

The JGNFC was a chance of a lifetime for us, and we will always treasure the experience.

Jeff and Maureen Harris

Jeff Gordon
Driver-Carolina Ford Dealers #1
Pittsboro, Ind. 46167

Copy of the original letter sent to Jeff Gordon by Maureen Harris.

Dear Mr. Gordon,

    I am an avid fan of yours. I would like to start a fan club on your behalf. I would also like to build in plastic, a model of your car and tractor-trailer rig. If you could supply me with any pictures of your vehicles I would greatly appreciate it. Also if we could keep in contact for information reguarding a fan club.

    Will you be a driver at the Copper Classic at Phoenix International Raceway Jan 30, 92 through Feb. 2, 92? My husband and I are going to be at that race. We would really like to visit with you.

    Our phone # is 602-936-8858, please call collect.

    Thank you for your help in getting the club started.

Sincerely,
Mrs. Maureen Harris

19   *Jeff Gordon: On A Chance*

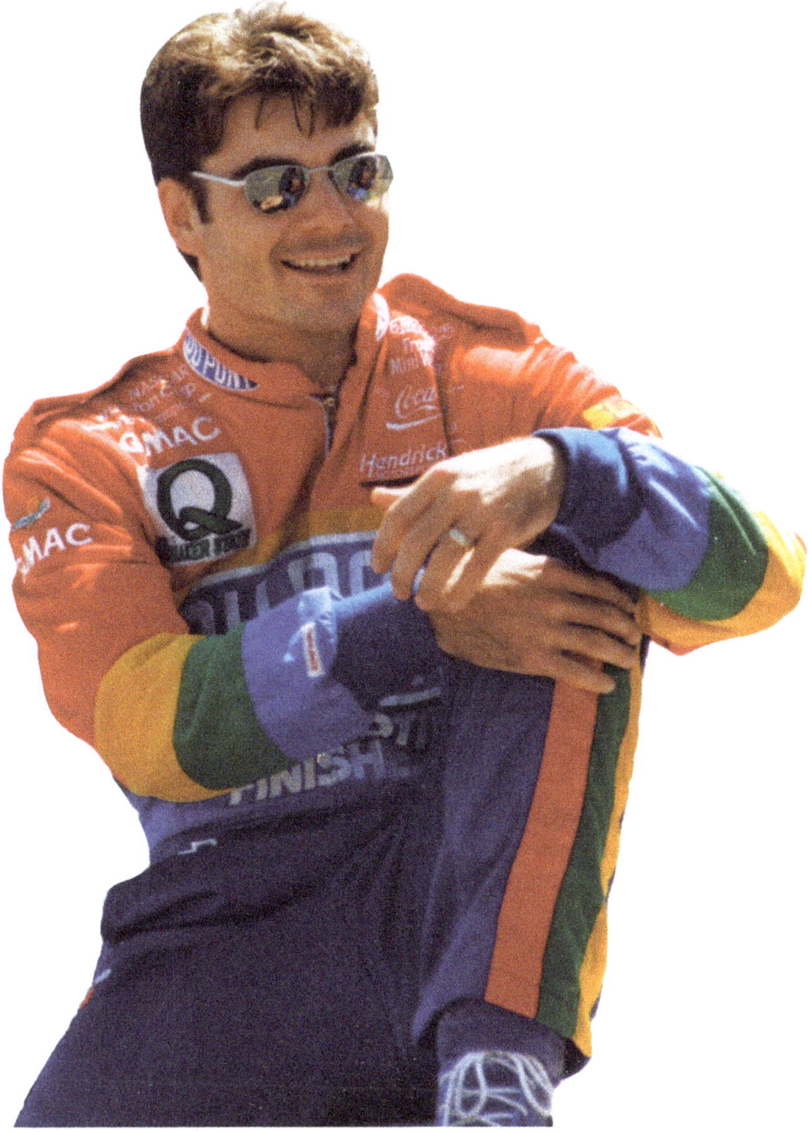

Jeff Gordon National Fan Club Events

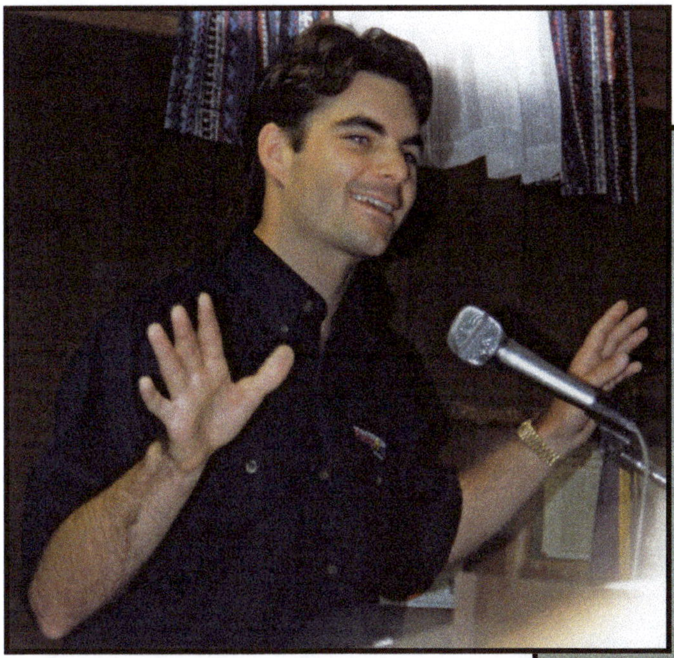

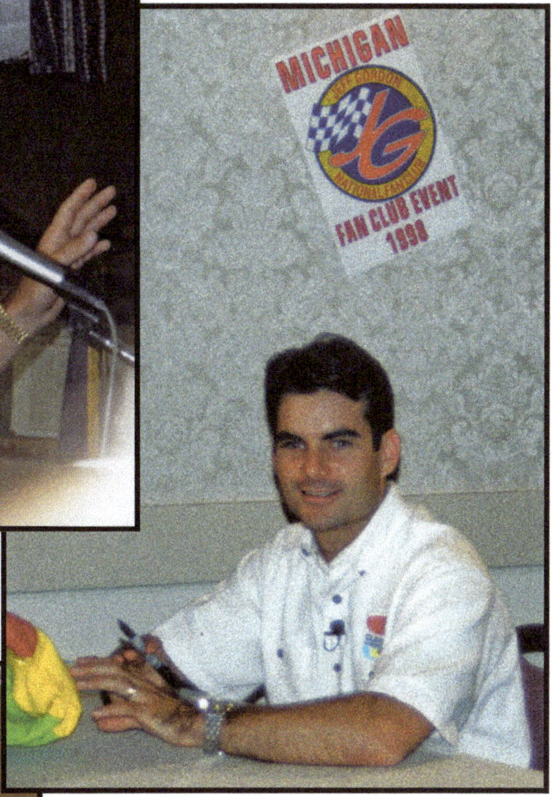
MICHIGAN
FAN CLUB EVENT
1998

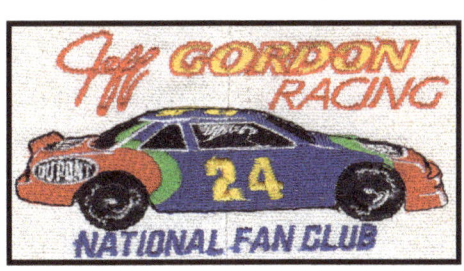

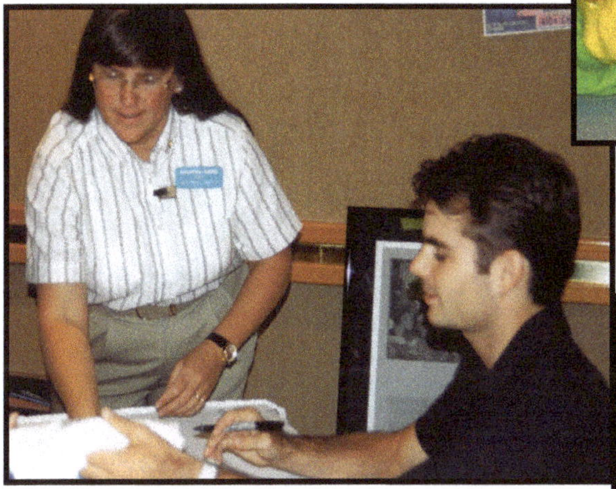

Jeff GORDON
RACING
24
NATIONAL FAN CLUB

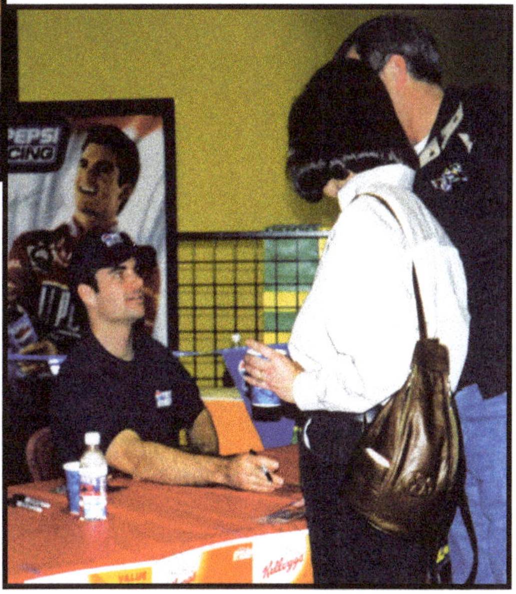

Fan Plates

Jeff Gordon: On A Chance

Fan Birthday Cakes

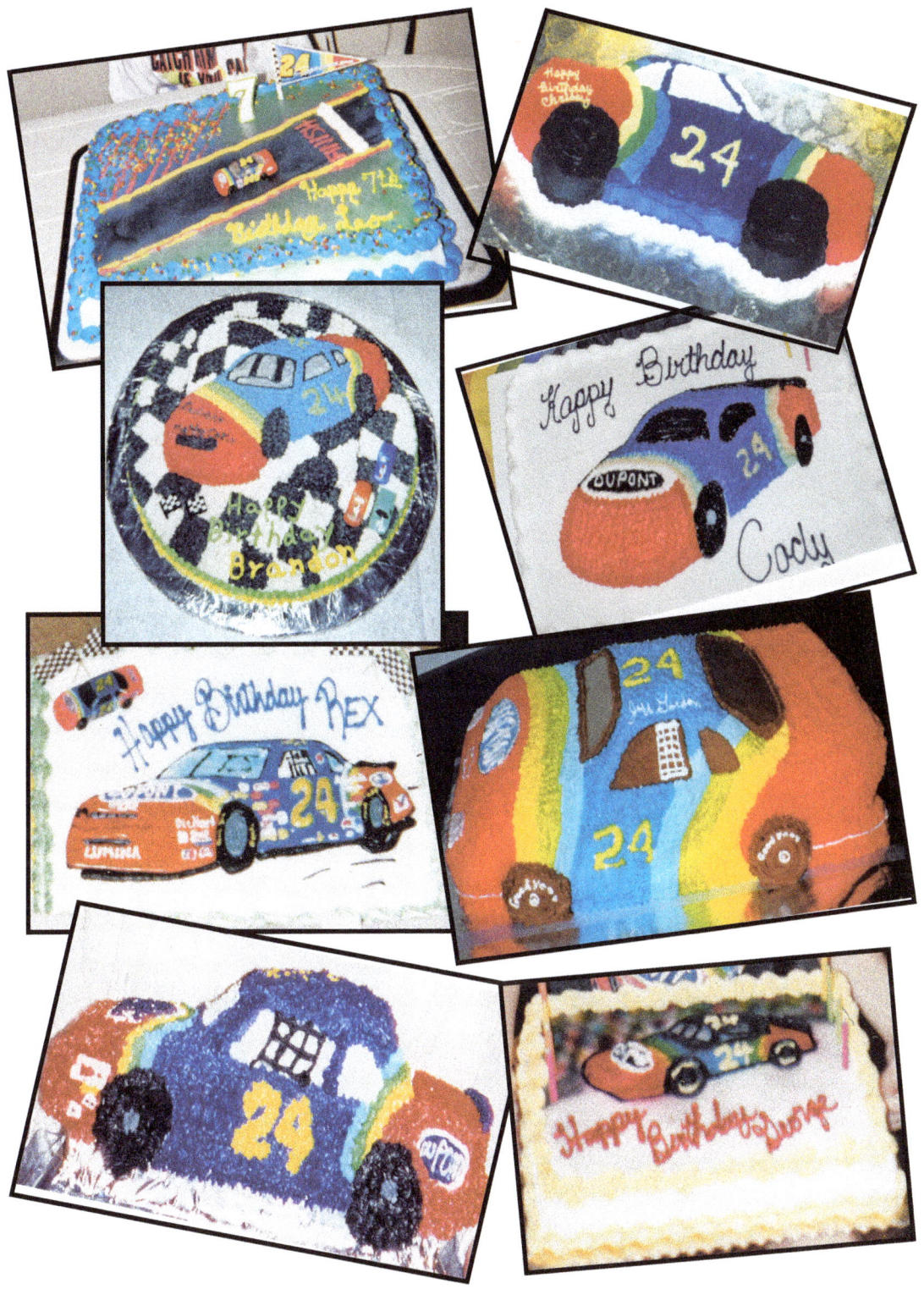

23   *Jeff Gordon: On A Chance*

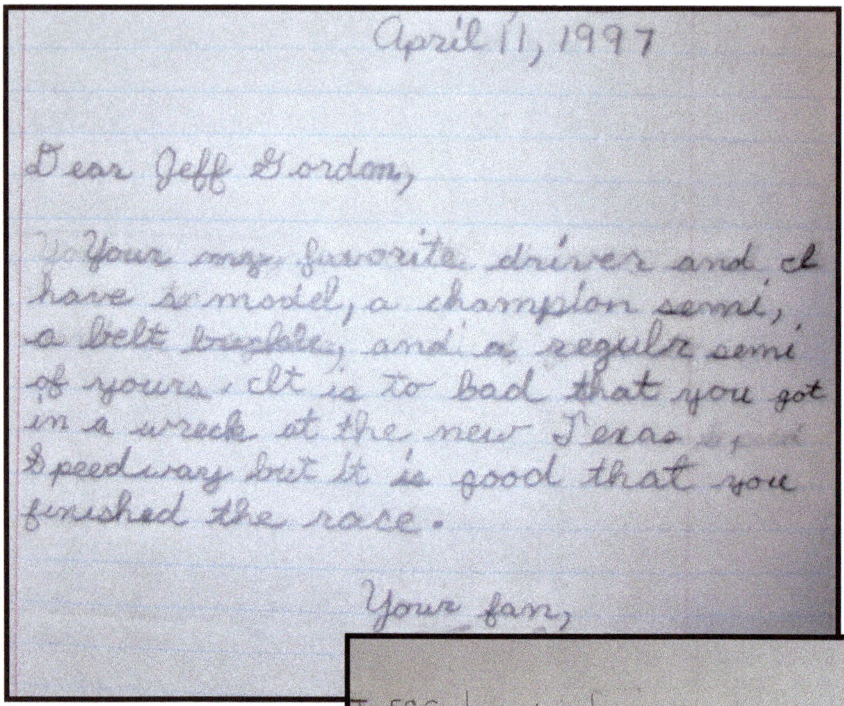

April 11, 1997

Dear Jeff Gordon,

Your my favorite driver and I have a model, a champion semi, a belt buckle, and a regular semi of yours. It is to bad that you got in a wreck at the new Texas Speedway but it is good that you finished the race.

Your fan,

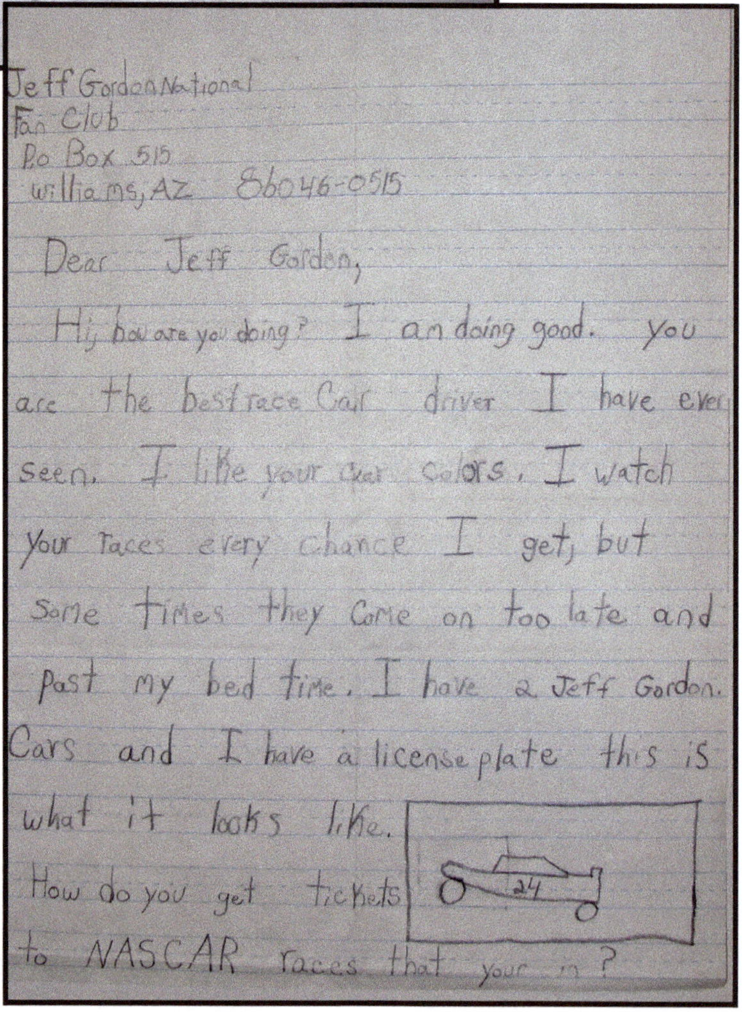

Jeff Gordon National
Fan Club
P.o Box 515
Williams, AZ 86046-0515

Dear Jeff Gordon,

Hi, how are you doing? I am doing good. You are the best race car driver I have ever seen. I like your car colors. I watch your races every chance I get, but some times they come on too late and past my bed time. I have a Jeff Gordon Cars and I have a license plate this is what it looks like. How do you get tickets to NASCAR races that your in?

Fan Mail

Influence for Youth

The amount of mail Jeff received from children was staggering. The modern-era race car driver has become such a role model to youth, that racing is now as recognizable as football & baseball.

Youngsters easily identify with the dazzle and colors of the modern-era racer's colorful uniform and their billboard race cars.

Jeff Gordon came into the NASCAR Cup series and brought youth; not only his youth, but youth from across the country. He also brought a new spark of young talent to, at the time, an under-recognized sport.

Jeff & Ray Evernham with young JGNFC members at a Fan Club Event.

Jeff, a born to race young man at the time he entered NASCAR, helped raise the level of the Cup series to an experience for the entire family. The letters he received from youngsters illustrated how he brought a lot of new young fans into racing.

Across the country many teachers use racing in the everyday classroom to help teach students in all avenues of learning, from the mathematics of keeping track of driver stats, to studying the intricacy of the race car. Requests for Jeff's schedule, stats, and other information about him and his motorsports career were sent to many schools across the United States.

Maureen Harris holding up Flat Stanley in the #24 Pit.

One day we received a letter from a young student asking us to show his Flat Stanley around the JGNFC office. No one in the office had ever seen a Flat Stanley. He is a character that school kids make out of paper and then color in their own, unique way. They are instructed to keep Flat Stanley with them and document their adventures together, or send him to family or friends for different journeys. Then the students must write a paper on Flat Stanley's adventures as a school project.

Upon receiving our first Flat Stanley, excitedly, Russ and I decided to take him with us to a race and fan club event. He went everywhere with us and had his photo taken on many occasions. Upon returning home we sent the young student a letter, chronicling Flat Stanley's trip, and included the photos we took.

Well, in doing so, several months after we mailed them, we began receiving Flat Stanleys from all over the country. To say the least, the numerous Flat Stanley visitors that continued to pour in, only got to stay within the JGNFC office.

Jeff has as much compassion for youth as he does for racing. The numerous letters he has received from youngsters who needed a positive role model, as well as from the ones who are struggling to fit in, are a testimony to how much children were attracted to Jeff when he entered into the major league series of racing.

Jeff Gordon: On A Chance

Jeff received a tremendous amount of mail from young race fans. Their letters and e-mails would express their friendship with Jeff and how they stood by him through all the ranting at their school by other students who supported their own favorite driver. But the young JG fan would stick with this newbie racer breaking into the biggest motorsports arena in the country.

Jeff's early stock car achievements, coupled with his youth, showed his young fans (and a lot of us adults) – that if you believe in your God, given talents and apply yourself, you too can excel "outside the box."

Left: A young JGNFC member shows Jeff his #24 haircut.

Right: Baby Jeff Gordon meets #24 driver Jeff Gordon.

I believe this was the first baby named after Jeff, and there would be many more to come.

Pictured here are some young JGNFC members, racing machines.

These show Jeff's positive influence on today's youth.

29 *Jeff Gordon: On A Chance*

"BOOMER"

In the early days the #24 Team named their race cars.

The JGNFC was honored to have a contest to name one of the #24 cars.

On the left is a plaque with a photo of "BOOMER" and the Rainbow Warriors.

The above plaque was awarded to the member who won the contest by coming up with the name of Boomer.

KIDS' CONTESTS

The JGNFC had plenty of coloring contests for the youth of the club.

Instead of a prize, they would receive their drawing back as a plaque, signed by Jeff.

This proved to be one of our most popular contests.

Jeff Gordon: On A Chance

Jeff Could You Please . . .

Jeff tried hard to be accessible and treated his fans as part of the 24 family. As a result, the influx of letters with requests of "Jeff, could you please stop by for . . . It will only take five minutes of your time." Or, "Jeff, can you please send us four race tickets to the Daytona 500?" "Jeff could you be in our wedding?"

There were tons of invitations to weddings, birthday parties, bar-b-que's, family reunions, Eagle Scout ceremonies, school events, and much more. If Jeff fulfilled all of the requests that flooded into the JGNFC office, he would never have time to drive a race car. Gotta love the race fans!

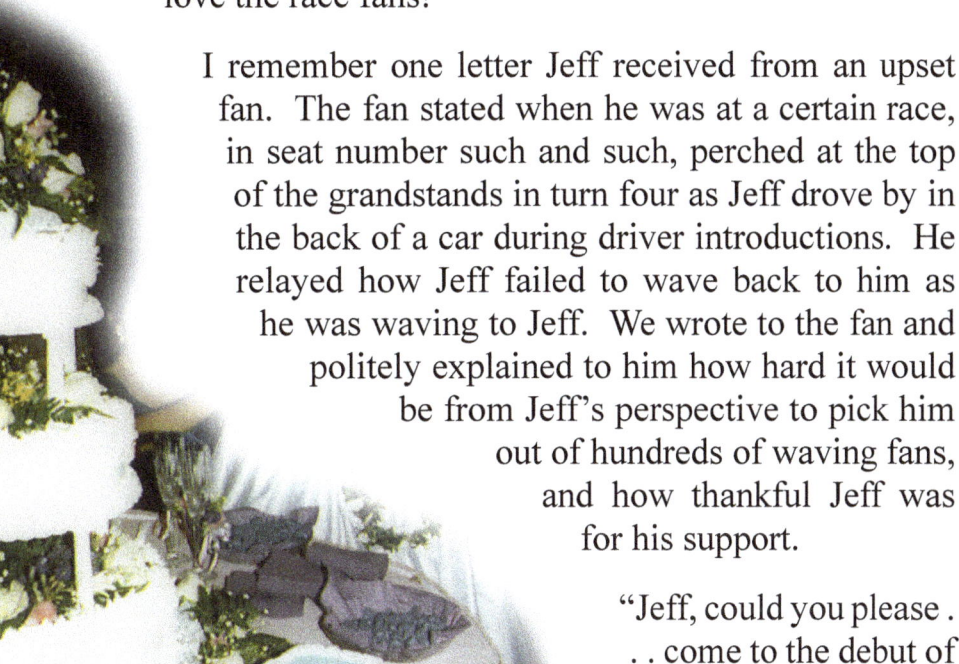

I remember one letter Jeff received from an upset fan. The fan stated when he was at a certain race, in seat number such and such, perched at the top of the grandstands in turn four as Jeff drove by in the back of a car during driver introductions. He relayed how Jeff failed to wave back to him as he was waving to Jeff. We wrote to the fan and politely explained to him how hard it would be from Jeff's perspective to pick him out of hundreds of waving fans, and how thankful Jeff was for his support.

"Jeff, could you please . . . come to the debut of our book, it will only take five minutes." (Just joking, Jeff!)

Up next . . . some actual letters sent in to Jeff.

Wedding cake and #24 Groom cake.

Letters for Jeff

Dear Jeff,
Thank you for being my favorite race car driver. You are the best driver I have ever known. I go to Calloway Elementary School. It's near the Franklin County Speedway. I would like to invite you over to my house some day before a race at Martinsville Speedway. If that don't work out it's okay, but I hope it does. I would like you to wright back to me and send me a picture of you and your car. Also one card with your signature on it. My birthday is August 19 and I'll be turning ten would you like to come and have a piece of cake that looks like your race car?
GOOD LUCK! racing.
Your race fan, David

Dear Jeff Gordon,
Hi my name is Nathaniel. I live in Marshall North Carolina. I am your biggest fan. And I mean your biggest fan! I've got t-shirts. Model cars. Hats. Posters. Rugs. And I keep track of your winnings. Good Luck!
Your friend
Nathaniel
P. S.
Please enclose an autograph. Oh and do you think you can pull some strings and get us 4 tickets to your next race at Bristol International Speedway. Please could you make them extra good seats. Please!!!!!

Dear Jeff Gordon,
We are writing this letter in hopes that it will reach you. Our father is a very big fan of yours. He has followed your career since day one. Our father is the type of man who helps others whenever possible. For years he has done without to help me and my sister. Our problem is every time he goes into a store he will go and look at your racing jackets and realize he can't afford one because of our financial problems.
We see the disappointment in his eyes every time. We don't have luxuries such as buying new clothes, dinning out or any other such luxuries. We were hoping you could help us thank our father for everything he does. He'd really appreciate a jacket. He wears an XL.
If there is anyway you could help us we would greatly be thankful. We can not purchase a jacket our selves because of our financial burdens. We hope you can help us out.
Thank you, Chris & Deb

Jeff Gordon: On A Chance

Dear Jeff,
Hello! What's up or down? Not to much around here. Just thought I would write you a letter. How's life treating you? Fine I hope. I was wondering if you would come to my wedding. I would be really honored and so would my fiance. Your presence at our wedding would make it really special. We haven't set a date yet but when we do I'll send you an invitation and directions. Thank you so very much for your time.
Sincerely, Loni

Dear Fan Club,
I wrote you back in March and I'm writing again because it is very important. I need to see if it is possible for Jeff Gordon to say Happy Birthday to my son. He has the same birthday and he loves Jeff Gordon. He will be 8 years old. All we are asking is during the race at one of the interviews with TV reporters if he would do this. Also wish my nephew Stephen & his wife happy health and congratulations on the birth of their daughter. She is due on the 4th too. This will mean so much to us.

Dear Mr. Gordon,
My name is Ricky, I'm 20. And I'm a very big fan of yours!
I mean, I think NASCAR should make you drive a fedex truck or blind fold you during races or something.
You know . . . to make it fair for everyone else.
Well anyway, I know your really busy, But, would you please send my girlfriend and her sister each an autographed photo?
I met you at Race Nite in Bristol and got one.
Thank you very much!
God bless.

Dear Jeff,
Hello my name is Melinda. The reason I'm writing you is because I'm a fan of yours and so is my fiance. He is one of your number 1 fans. This is how big of a fan he is of yours. We are getting married on Feb. 24, because of your car number. He also want's a NASCAR groom cake of your car.

Also for our honeymoon we are coming to see you race in North Carolina at Rockingham. I was just wondering if you would send him something special like tickets to see you in the pits. But if you can't that's OK. He would like it a lot if you send him something.
Thanks A lot, Melinda

Special Needs Requests

This should be called "behind the scenes" because Jeff received a tremendous number of requests for autographed donations and special needs situations.

Since we began working with him, Jeff has provided an endless supply of autographed items to charities, fund raisers and numerous causes. In certain instances, we allowed fans who were ill to attend a fan club meeting in order to get the chance to visit with Jeff.

There is an off track side of Jeff that many fans are unable to see. Jeff is actually a very humble and caring person. His immense love for people enabled him to give from his heart.

I remember in Jeff's early years in the Cup Series, how he was criticized for not doing charitable things. Unbeknownst to the media and public, his contributions were usually behind the scenes, done strictly from the heart.

There was an early incident where Jeff was mobbed by fans at the racetrack. They were handing items over a fence for him to sign. As Jeff was signing autographs, a very young kid climbed the fence to give him something to sign. The kid lost his balance and ended up ripping a gash in his arm. Jeff was devastated that the young fan was injured and stated that he couldn't sign any more autographs for fear of another injury. Jeff was criticized in the media for discontinuing autographs for his fans, but there was no mention of the young kid getting hurt. Jeff showed more compassion for his fans that day than he was given credit for.

Jeff received tons of heart wrenching letters; even we found it hard to see how he handled the tremendous pressures of providing some kind of temporary relief to fans who were grieving a setback in life. The demand on these race car drivers, turned superstars, to bring a bit of joy for the unique circumstances in the lives of their fans was usually handled behind the scenes.

You Want What Signed?

You would think that the modern-era driver was "John Hancock" with the overwhelming number of items sent in to be autographed.

Our personal favorites were the youngsters who sifted through their treasure trove of trading cards, picked out their favorite JG card, took the time to write a letter, and then mailed it off for a signature. You could almost feel as though the child were in victory circle when the autographed card came back from Jeff.

After processing Jeff's mail at the JGNFC office, it was then shipped off for him to sign. It is amazing the amount of items Jeff received for a signature. In the early years, fans would send in a stack of 25 to 30 cards at a time. That amount coming from thousands of fans would quickly add up, so the limit had to be set at 2 items per person. We were told about how the fans would be upset and not abide by that rule. Most fans sending in items didn't realize the tremendous number of requests Jeff was receiving on a daily basis and each felt they were most likely the only one sending in something at that particular time. Once you explained to the fans about the overwhelming number of items coming in for Jeff, they became very understanding and patient enough to wait the time limit for their favorite driver's signature. By far, Jeff's fans are some of the most understanding we have ever met.

Besides receiving thousands of items through the mail, Jeff autographed some unique collectibles at the JGNFC events. A few of the unique items signed were a front door, vehicle motors, shirts people were wearing, and handmade items, among others.

Jeff would sign bare arms or hands to be used as a template for a tattoo. At one event, a lady flung her leg onto the table and wanted him to sign her leg, so she could get it tattooed.

Over the years, the fans never failed to inform Jeff exactly where they wanted his signature to go on their favorite collectible. In some of the instructions received through the mail, it would include a sticky with an arrow pointing to the exact location the fan wanted to be signed or sometimes a much lengthier message was included within the letter. You name it and Jeff signed it.

A JGNFC member's dog had several blankets autographed!

Jeff Gordon: On A Chance

Some pretty awesome #24 paint jobs.

Top:
Cement Mixer

Right:
Yes, even a refrigerator!

Bottom:
A cardboard car.

#24 paint jobs.

Above: Taxi Cab

Middle: VW Bug

Bottom: 4X4

Jeff Gordon: On A Chance

Connecting With Jeff

Gifts were often included in the mounds of mail that Jeff received. Some items sent to Jeff included lucky pennies, four leaf clovers, photographs of fans with their massive collections of JG memorabilia or dressed in their entire JG garb. Jeff received books, poems, songs written for him, information about babies named after him, as well as family pets. He received favorite Matchbox/Hotwheels cars from young fans, and even received some Lucky Charms cereal to bring him good fortune at the race track. Of course, by the time the plastic bag of cereal reached us, it was pretty crushed up.

Photos of fans poured in showing couples who centered their wedding themes on racing and Jeff Gordon. Some of the mail we received told how some fans were buried with their favorite JG item. And, yes, fans have included Jeff's car or number on many cemetery headstones. At the JGNFC we also received letters about last wills of fans who included their season track passes as part of their estate. That is how dedicated the average racing fan is towards their favorite driver.

One of the most unique forms of mail that we ever received for Jeff was the vegetable and fruit mail! For many weeks a fan sent in a decorative fruit or vegetable every one of which had a different composition on it. The post office was quite amused and surprisingly each one was delivered without a problem. That was ingenuity to the greatest extent! Leave it to us crazy race fans to come up with something like that. We all, including Jeff, enjoyed the weekly prose on each piece.

After the famous Pepsi commercial about Jeff needing a cup holder in his race car, we received tons of cup holders in the mail to give to Jeff. In my opinion, that turned out to be one of the fans most favorite commercials.

If Jeff expressed a desire or need for anything special during an interview, we would receive many gifts for him as a result of his comments. He would also get letters from the fans on how to set up the #24 race car, how to drive around each race track, what to wear, which driver he should stay away from that week, and how to style his hair. Yes Jeff, I believe that was your #1 suggestion from race fans.

Cards flooded in on Jeff's birthday, Valentine's Day, and holidays. Some other items mailed to Jeff included resumes for employment, requests to become a team member, angel pins, handmade pillows, quilts, and more. Young kids sent in their school sports trading card in exchange for an autographed hero card. We even had a young member send Jeff his lucky rock. Jeff truly appreciated all the dedicated support not only from his most beloved JGNFC fans, but all race fans.

As Jeff's popularity soared, the letters inquiring about being related to him poured in. In one letter, a fan tried to find every way to be related to Jeff. She stated something to the effect that she was the twelfth cousin of Jeff's sixth cousin on his mother's side. We had to politely write her back and suggest to her to go through her family to see if there was a connection to the Gordon family.

One morning a lady entered our office. She was from a nearby city and was wearing a brand new JG shirt. Jeff had just won one of his Winston Millions events. She heard him during a post race interview say that he wanted to share his winnings by giving some away to charity. She informed us that she was there to collect some of the money he was going to give away. Once we informed her about the channels on how Jeff disperses his charitable contributions, she said, "Well, if I can't get any of the money, what am I going to do with this new shirt I just bought?" She immediately turned and proceeded to storm out of the office before we could give her the address of Jeff's charitable foundation.

Through the years of mail, packages, e-mail, phone calls, fan club events, and interaction with the fans, we thought we had heard and seen it all. But then something would arrive -- or happen -- which provided affirmation that race fans can conjure up just about anything when their desire to connect with Jeff is strong. It was always fun when that next unusual request for Jeff Gordon or that quirky letter arrived at the JGNFC office. In all our years of processing Jeff's fan mail, there was nothing quite as entertaining as the fruit and vegetable mail.

The Fruit & Vegetable Mail

In my opinion, the most unusual and coolest items we received for Jeff was the fruit and vegetable mail. A fan from Texas sent to Jeff a piece of artificial fruit or a vegetable for many weeks.

Everyone at the JGNFC was surprised how the unique mail made it through the postal service unscathed and with stamps intact. It became such a delight to receive and read the clever prose inscribed on each piece.

Because this is so extraordinary, I would like to share a few pieces and their prose with you. I hope you enjoy them as much as Jeff and the JGNFC staff did.

HOT PEPPER:
Dear Jeff Gordon,
You & the #24 DuPont Chevy Team are really hot stuff! From your absolute biggest fan ever!

BANANA:
Dear Jeff Gordon,
I go bananas when you crash!! I still believe in you. Good luck & God bless! From your absolute biggest fan ever!

BELL PEPPER:
Dear Jeff Gordon,
BELLS rang, people cheered, and time stood still when you won at New Hampshire! You are really some kind of awesome, and so is the #24 team. Good luck & God bless! From your absolute biggest fan ever!

Jeff Gordon: On A Chance

POTATO:
Dear Jeff Gordon,
Even though all "eyes" were on you & the 24 team this weekend, you handled it great! Way to go at Dover! Good luck & God bless! From your absolute biggest fan ever!

SQUASH:
Dear Jeff Gordon,
It was really great seeing you squash everyone at Watkins Glen! Good luck & may God bless! Your absolute biggest fan ever!

CARROT:
Dear Jeff Gordon,
You're a real 24 carrot driver! Good luck & God Bless. From your absolute biggest fan ever!

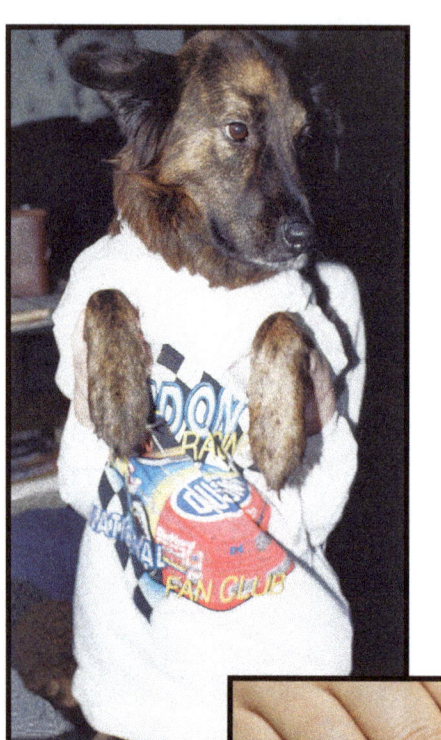

Left: A dog in a Jeff Gordon shirt? The JGNFC member's dog is showing off his race day attire.

Middle: One of the many nail designs.

Bottom Left: A #24 leg tattoo.

Bottom Right: Another fan favorite was the #24 carved pumpkins!

Members sent in some pretty clever photographs of Halloween pumpkin carvings

And some of the biggest *fanatics* were kids dressed up in a Jeff Gordon costume for Halloween.

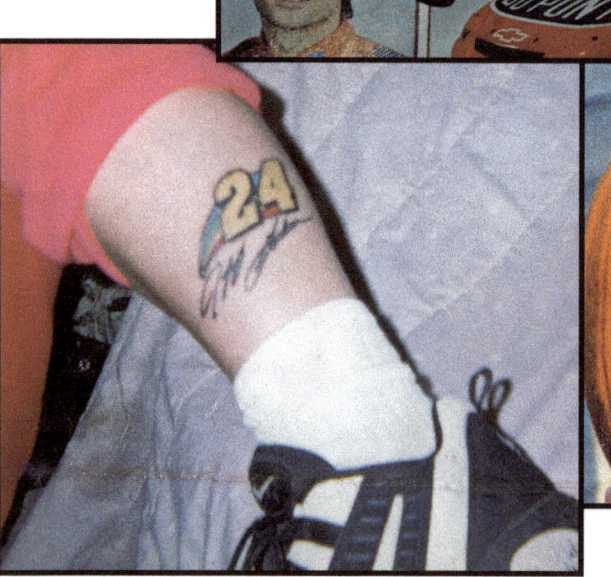

Jeff Gordon: On A Chance

Left: Jeff holding a hand painted coconut that was given to him by a young JGNFC member at a 1996 fan club event.

The young man did an awesome job with his talent out of love for his favorite driver!

Jeff Gordon: On A Chance 46

Personal Experiences

When we first met Jeff in the early 1990's he was a humble and somewhat shy young man in person. But on the race track, he was a racer through and through. Watching him race open wheel cars, and then stock cars, it was an instant attraction to this kid in his teens. He was literally a pedal to the metal race car driver.

Let's take a walk in our shoes as we share some of our favorite personal moments during our tenure with the Jeff Gordon National Fan Club.

When the #24 team came to test at Phoenix International Raceway, Russ made lunch for the team. He cooked up a pot of homemade chili which was warmly embraced because it happened to be a cold day.

It was a pleasure to meet the new team. They had a simple white hauler with the DuPont logo on the side. Jeff's team was there with other cup drivers and also Mario Andretti, which was a special thrill for Russ because Mario was one of his favorite Indy car drivers.

At one of the first races we attended, a team member asked what was the one thing, as fans, we most wanted to do. Russ mentioned that he always longed to go on top of a race trailer. In racing this is a normal part of the crew and drivers, daily routine, but to the fan a treat. His request allowed them to see a different perspective of what was special and exciting for the average race fan. And, yes, we did get to go on top of the race trailer. What a cool view!

One morning when we arrived at the race track, we were supposed to receive garage passes. Because of a mix-up, the passes wouldn't be ready until the following day. Therefore, we thought if we could make our way into the garage and to Jeff's trailer, we could stay around the race trailer. The passes would allow us to come and go into the garage area as we wanted for the rest of the race weekend.

Russ and I thought, "Okay, how is this supposed to work?" Getting into a NASCAR garage area without passes, past security, past the "red shirts"? (Back then a red shirt was our nickname for NASCAR officials.) This was during a time when security within the garage area was minimal. This particular day was a Thursday and the race happened to be in Phoenix.

Phoenix Raceway Testing 1992

Right: Kenny Schrader, Ray Evernham and Jeff looking over testing results.

Left: Jeff in #24 test car.

Right: Russ Harris serving the #24 team chili for lunch.

Jeff Gordon: On A Chance

Right: Mario Andretti was also at PIR testing when Jeff and the Hendrick teams were there.

Below:
First #24 DuPont Team Hauler.

49   Jeff Gordon: On A Chance

Back then a Thursday meant that the security was not as tight as the days closer to race day. The attitude of the gate guards would later be of assistance to us.

We arrived to the interior section of the race track without a problem. As we approached the garage entry gate, there was a security guard on each side. What were we to do now? We began to plan on what we were going to say that would sound convincing enough to let us enter the garage. As we were standing there discussing our strategy, the "fan angels" looked favorably upon us.

Russ Harris & Jeff discuss fan relations at the track.

It was like a scene right out of a Hollywood movie! A young kid was riding his bicycle by the gate. The bike tires slipped when he drove into a nearby gravel area. He and his bicycle toppled to the ground. Screaming as he fell, the two guards ran over to assist him. We didn't even look at one another, as we seemed to know that the opportunity was ours for the taking!

Acting like we knew what we were doing, we slipped through the gate. After entering the garage area we got to the team hauler, and ended up hanging around Jeff's trailer the rest of the day enjoying this new adventure. That event was like the old saying, "When opportunity knocks, be there to take advantage of it!"

Another neat experience was during a race weekend in Charlotte, NC. We were attending a function for the announcement of the Race Rock Restaurant located in Orlando, Florida. Afterward there was going to be a reception in the suites of the Charlotte Motor Speedway, and Jeff invited us to attend. How were we going to get inside the prestigious suite area of Charlotte Motor Speedway?

Once again, we had to act like we knew what we were doing. After all, would any fan pass up a chance to get inside a reception of that magnitude? We would always conduct ourselves in a manner that reflected the respect and admiration we have for Jeff, and that which he has always given us. But you have to realize that even though we were working on Jeff's behalf, we were still race fans who enjoyed the insider's experience.

Track security manned the door where the reception was held. We handed the guard one of our cards and stated that we were invited to attend the reception with Jeff Gordon. Once again, here was that divine help arriving from the "fan angels." The security guard looked at us, looked at the card, and finally after a bit of a pause said, "Go ahead." Yes, it was meant to be!

We took the elevator up and arrived ahead of the scheduled start time. Since we had never been to this type of racing function, we did not know what to expect. We were still dressed in nice casual clothes from the previous event. Much to our chagrin, as people began arriving, we noticed they were dressed in evening gowns and much more than casual dress. Did we ever feel embarrassed!

We started to make a quiet exit, just as Jeff walked in. The ever cordial person that he is, he never missed a beat and made his way over to greet us. We exchanged greetings, talked a bit, and then made our exit. It was such a delight to see another part of the racing scene.

In the early days of the JGNFC, Jeff taped a recording for our answering machine. Shortly after he made the message, we started getting hang up calls. This went on for many weeks, and then all at once they stopped. A short period of time went by when we got a call from a gentleman who wanted to know what the association was with the number he was calling. We explained to him what the JGNFC was. He thanked us and hung up.

He called back several days later and informed us that the hang up calls we had been receiving were from his young daughter and her friend. He was out of town for a length of time and when he got home he noticed a number of long distance calls to our number on his bill. After calling us he confronted his daughter and was told how she and her girlfriend would call just to hear Jeff's voice. However, when we answered they would hang up because they were embarrassed. After the father apologized for any inconvenience they may have caused, we expressed to him that the incident was not a problem for us, and how cute it was that the girls wanted to hear Jeff. Both girls remained members of the JGNFC for many years.

While attending a pole night event in Charlotte, and still being fresh to the biggest league in racing, I did a funny thing. Jeff ended up winning the pole that night, which was a big event. As he crossed the finish line with a track record time, I jumped right over the pit wall with the team. In my excitement after a few high fives, I realized what I had done and scurried back over the wall before the "red shirts" caught me. I was embarrassed at the time, but later reveled in a once in a lifetime experience of being over the wall on a hot pit road! Fans will know what I mean when I say, "Pretty cool!"

My most treasured experience with Jeff was after a fan club event. Jeff was dropped off and needed a ride after the event. Guess who got to give him a lift? Yes, I did! After the meeting, our JGNFC manager and I pulled out of the event location, with Jeff giving directions in the backseat. He directed me across four lanes of traffic to make a left hand turn. As we approached the traffic light, he remembered that you cannot make a left turn at that particular light. He apologized and then proceeded to tell me to go back across four lanes of traffic and turn right. Stating that we would be able to flip a U-turn on a side street.

Have you ever had a backseat driver telling you to fly across four lanes of oncoming traffic? And that it was clear while shouting out, "Go, go, go!" Well, I did, and it was Jeff Gordon! Instead of yelling, "We are gonna get creamed!" I put my faith in one of the best race car drivers in the world. Darting across four lanes of traffic, I made a right turn, and eventually got Jeff safely to his destination. It may not have been a big deal to Jeff, but how many fans can say they gave Jeff a lift?

Early in Jeff's career, he told us how he once tried to open up a bag of Skittles candy in the race car. Only Jeff Gordon can be driving approximately 150 miles per hour and try to open a bag of candy! Fumbling with the bag while wearing thick racing gloves, he ripped open the bag, and Skittles went flying throughout the race car. Jeff continued to recount how he managed to eat a few; but the rest drove him crazy as at every turn he could see them rolling around on the floor of the race car.

Maureen & Russ Harris with crew chief Ray Evernham in victory circle at Pocono Raceway.

Another favorite race memory was at Pocono Raceway. Jeff had been leading the race all day. The race was nearing the end as small amounts of rain began falling. Quite often because of the size of a race track it can be raining at one end and not the other. Jeff radioed to crew chief Ray Evernham about the rain. Ray radioed back and told him no, that those were bugs. Jeff responded back, "No, they are rain drops." Once again, Ray radioed back saying they were bugs. This conversation went on a few more times, until Ray said, "No, Jeff, those are bugs. You are way out ahead of everyone else. You only have ten laps to go. Those are bugs." Jeff quickly responded, "Oh yeah. I guess those are bugs!"

This was humorous because Jeff was way out in front of the pack and did not restart well at the time. So Ray didn't want a caution that would guarantee another restart and could take away the opportunity to stay out front during the last few laps.

We had several opportunities to experience victory circle with the #24 team. One of those times, after all the photo shoots, Ray asked us to take the winner's trophy to the race hauler. He also let us keep one of the opened bottles of champagne and Jeff's Gatorade sweat towel.

As we walked from victory circle through the garage area, we had to pass by the fans viewing area. The cheers and offers to take the trophy off our hands poured in as we proudly continued our trek to escort the trophy to the race trailer. Such a neat experience for us, as JG fans.

While attending the inaugural race at Texas in 1997, the #24 crew manager Andy Papathanassiou asked Russ to help out as an honorary crew member. They were short until some of the other crew members arrived. Russ was anxious to have a dream come true. He went with Andy to get instructions for his part on the #24 crew.

Russ was instructed to stay behind the wall and catch the tires that would be rolled to him during pit stops. As Russ was bending over the wall to see exactly how this should be done, Jeff was involved in an accident on the front stretch. Russ and Andy looked up just as Jeff's car came flying through the grass, and stopped close to where they stood in the pit!

So much for his short lived participation as a member of the #24 pit crew. Then again, how many fans can say they had the honor of being a member of Jeff's pit crew?

Our 10+ years of providing fan services through the JGNFC was one of the most exciting periods of our life. As race fans, we had the opportunity to walk where many fans would love to walk. We were fortunate to have some great memories, and shared some funny fan times. Every day we treasured the experiences with Jeff and the family of fans we met along our journey. My heartfelt thanks go out again to Jeff, Carol, and John for giving us the chance of a lifetime.

Jeff & crew chief Ray Evernham as they head for the garage after crashing in Texas.

Jeff spinning at Texas Motor Speedway in 1997. This happened right in front of our pit location. We almost had the car in our lap!

Thanks, Jeff, for all the JGNFC appearances!

The events were the highlights of the fan experience!

Jeff Gordon: On A Chance

Fun Photos!

Left: Jeff tries out a police motorcycle after a JGNFC fan club event in California.

Above: Race Rock contributors (left to right), Richard Petty, Michael Andretti, Bobby Moore, John Force & Jeff Gordon. (Feb 1996)

Above: Our friends who managed the souvenir trailers were frequent visitors to the JGNFC office. We always enjoyed their visits. Once in awhile they would open up and let the locals purchase fan gear. Everyone in the area loved seeing the trucks arrive, as it was hard finding racing items in northern Arizona.

Jeff Gordon: On A Chance

The wonderful people who toured Jeff's #24 Super Truck came by the JGNFC office for a visit.

I was able to drive the race truck on Route 66 in Williams, AZ. What a blast!

It was easy getting in, but now comes the hard part . . . getting out! No door, you say? Oh, goodie!

OK, Jeff, tell me again? What is the gracious way of getting out of a race truck?

Meeting Other Drivers

Left: Maureen Harris & Ernie Irvan in the garage.

Below: With Tony Stewart.

Wow!
Meeting the Pettys
Middle Left: Kyle Petty
Above: Richard Petty
Bottom Left: Adam Petty

Jeff Gordon: On A Chance

Top Left: Maureen & A.J. Foyt

Top Right: Lake Speed did not mind taking his photo with JGNFC office staff.

Right: Maureen & Kenny Schrader

Left:
With Davey Allison in 1992. We were laughing because my husband was a klutz with the camera.

Around The Garage

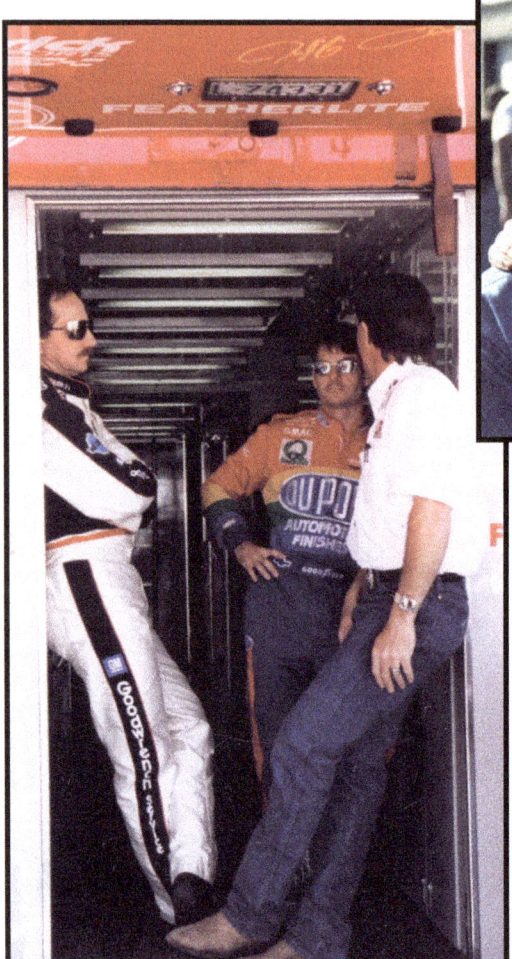

Above: Ernie Irvan & Ricky Craven.

Above:
Dale Earnhardt and Jeff inside the #24 race trailer

Right:
Mark Martin, Jeff, and Crew Chief Ray Evernham

Jeff Gordon: On A Chance

Victory Circle Memories

63   Jeff Gordon: On A Chance

Pit Road

Pit Road ~ one of the most exhilarating parts of the race experience!

Jeff Gordon: On A Chance   64

65   *Jeff Gordon: On A Chance*

Jeff Gordon: On A Chance

JGNFC Collectibles

During the years of the Jeff Gordon National Fan Club we were able to produce some neat fan club collectibles, which were always a big hit with the members. The most popular collectible was the monthly newsletter, which was the largest motorsports fan newsletter ever published.

The JGNFC newsletter took two weeks to create. We encouraged members to submit anything related to Jeff Gordon for publication. Between Jeff and the fans, there was always enough input to fill the 16-page monthly newsletter. The most premium pages were the front and back, as members were eager for their photos to appear on these pages.

The newsletter became so popular that fans told us they could not wait for it to arrive each month. If it was late, the calls flooded into our office.

Jeff Gordon: On A Chance

JGNFC Newsletters:
The JGNFC newsletter began with Issue #1 Vol #1 in April 1992. It started as an 8-page newsletter with a color BGN Series Baby Ruth masthead, and soon grew into 16 pages.

When Jeff began racing in the Cup Series, the newsletter masthead switched to the #24 masthead.

We had many fans tell us that they joined just because of the monthly newsletter. It became the most popular fan newsletter of the NASCAR series.

JGNFC 1993 Metal Trading Cards: (Shown on page 72.)
The set of Metal Trading Cards were one of the first JGNFC collectibles. With permission from the Gordon family, we secured some early photos of Jeff for this one of a kind card set.

JGNFC Trading Card: (Photo below.)
With the help of the wonderful people at Press Pass, the JGNFC issued as part of it's membership packet, an exclusive fan club trading card.

JGNFC Logo T-shirt:
The JGNFC produced several T-shirts that were available to the members. And with the creation of the new logo in 1996, the JGNFC began producing a special member T-shirt.

JGNFC Logo Patch:
A very well created embroidered patch of the JGNFC logo.

Below: Glass Mug

Right: JGNFC Patch

Right: JGNFC Hero Card

JGNFC Logo Hats:
Two hats were developed with the first logo and then with the JGNFC circle logo. Both were made of high quality embroidery.

JGNFC Logo Button & Lapel Pin:
The JGNFC produced a logo button and lapel pin. Due to their popularity, we could not keep these in stock.

JGNFC Logo Glass Mugs:
Personalized etched glass mugs. Various colors of blue, green, and crystal.

JGNFC Hero Cards:
The JGNFC included a 5X7 Club Hero Card within the member packets.

JGNFC Calling Card: (Photo on page 71.)
Limited Edition calling card by Finish Line Racing. The cards sold out within a short period of time, and were the only JGNFC calling card produced.

JGNFC Fan Flag:
High quality silk screened large JGNFC logo fan flag.

JGNFC 1/64th Die-Cast Cars:
One of the most sought after collectibles was our 1/64 JGNFC die-cast car. Thanks to the help of the fine people at Action Performance we put out a series of JGNFC cars from 1993 to 1999.

Jeff Gordon National Fan Club
1/64th scale Die Cast cars.

Below:
JGNFC Bumper Sticker

Jeff Gordon: On A Chance

JGNFC Bumper Sticker:
The JGNFC bumper sticker was a big hit.

JGNFC Jacket: (Photos of Jeff with jacket on ~ Pages 66 & 74.)
A nice windbreaker jacket with JGNFC logo on the front and a large embroidered logo on the back.

Two types of JGNFC hats.
Right: The first design.
Below: JGNFC embroidered circle logo hat.

Right: JGNFC Finish Line Racing Calling Card Limited Edition.

Jeff Gordon: On A Chance

Jeff GORDON RACING
NATIONAL FAN CLUB

"THE YOUNG YEARS"
SERIES 1
LIMITED TO 1200 SETS

Quarter Midget - Junior Novice Division
Jeff is 5 years old, weighs 36 lbs., and is 44" tall.
The trophy he won was 48" tall. He couldn't carry it.
July 4th weekend, 1977. Sunnyvale, California.
Baylands Quarter Midget Track. Western States
Championship race. Jeff's first big win. He's wearing a Simpson Driving Suit said to be the smallest ever made by Simpson.

LICENSED BY: JEFF GORDON NATIONAL FAN CLUB
P.O. BOX 515
WILLIAMS, AZ 86046-0515
PHONE 602-JEFF

JGNFC Metal Card Set of 3.

Photos used on the cards are courtesy of the Gordon Family.

Jeff Gordon: On A Chance

JGNFC Logo Leather Jacket:
The JGNFC all leather jacket was a copy of the windbreaker. Custom made to order by Wolf Designs. JGNFC logo on front and large logo on the back.

Jeff is wearing the JGNFC leather Jacket at the 1997 Pocono, PA fan club event.

73   Jeff Gordon: On A Chance

www.hobopublishing.com

www.MaureenHarris.net

Jeff Gordon: On A Chance 74

www.ingramcontent.com/pod-product-compliance
Lightning Source LLC
LaVergne TN
LVHW070948070426
835507LV00028B/3450